M000197083

positive
vibes

positive
vibes

INSPIRING THOUGHTS
FOR CHANGE AND
TRANSFORMATION

gordon smith

HAY HOUSE

Australia • Canada • Hong Kong • India
South Africa • United Kingdom • United States

First published and distributed in the United Kingdom by:
Hay House UK Ltd, 292B Kensal Road, London W10 5BE
Tel.: (44) 20 8962 1230; Fax: (44) 20 8962 1239.
www.hayhouse.co.uk

Published and distributed in the United States of America by:
Hay House, Inc., PO Box 5100, Carlsbad, CA 92018-5100.
Tel.: (1) 760 431 7695 or (800) 654 5126; Fax: (1) 760 431 6948 or
(800) 650 5115.
www.hayhouse.com

Published and distributed in Australia by:
Hay House Australia Ltd, 18/36 Ralph St, Alexandria NSW 2015.
Tel.: (61) 2 9669 4299; Fax: (61) 2 9669 4144.
www.hayhouse.com.au

Published and distributed in the Republic of South Africa by:
Hay House SA (Pty), Ltd, PO Box 990, Witkoppen 2068.
Tel./Fax: (27) 11 467 8904. www.hayhouse.co.za

Published and distributed in India by:
Hay House Publishers India, Muskaan Complex, Plot No.3, B-2,
Vasant Kunj, New Delhi - 110 070. Tel.: (91) 11 4176 1620;
Fax: (91) 11 4176 1630.
www.hayhouse.co.in

Distributed in Canada by:
Raincoast, 9050 Shaughnessy St, Vancouver, BC V6P 6E5.
Tel.: (1) 604 323 7100; Fax: (1) 604 323 2600

Text © Gordon Smith, 2013

The moral rights of the author have been asserted.

All rights reserved. No part of this book may be reproduced by any
mechanical, photographic or electronic process, or in the form of a
phonographic recording; nor may it be stored in a retrieval system,
transmitted or otherwise be copied for public or private use, other
than for 'fair use' as brief quotations embodied in articles and reviews,
without prior written permission of the publisher.

A catalogue record for this book is available from the British Library.

ISBN: 978-1-4019-4266-3

Certified Chain of Custody
Promoting Sustainable Forestry
www.sfiprogram.org
SFI-01268

SUSTAINABLE
FORESTRY
INITIATIVE

SFI label applies to the text stock

There is no more positive energy in the world than the force of a loving pet.

I dedicate this little book of upliftment to my spaniel, Princess Meg, for the unconditional love that never fails to bring joy to all who meet her.

contents

*B*eing positive in the face of adversity always works for me; why not allow it to work for you?

It is my hope that this little book will inspire you and help you to connect to your inner spirit and move forward, whatever is happening in your life.

May all your vibes be positive.

With love,

Beginnings

Whenever I come to a new episode in my life I try to remind myself of how I used to feel when I had fear inside me, and any thought of change shot terror through my entire being. Now I welcome change with open arms, as I know that with every new direction on my journey there will be excitement to experience, as well as new lessons to learn, new people to meet, and sometimes new places and situations to encounter. With all of that, what is there to fear?

*T*oday is the first day of a new journey.

Put positive energy into your first footstep and good things will follow.

*D*irection is essential when you set out on a journey. Life is the greatest journey you will ever make, so pay attention to where you are headed.

$\mathcal{S}$omething has changed overnight and it is right to feel excited about what is to come.

*W*hen the snow covers the ground in winter it's easy to believe that nothing is happening beneath. But in the ground below there is preparation for better days.

Be like the earth and get ready, for the best is yet to come.

The spring skies are filled with the sound of birdsong. There is a message in it for you if you take the time to listen to it.

This is one of those days when something is telling you to go forward. That voice is your higher self, the self that knows.

*I*t's never too late to start something.

Aspirations aren't only for the young.

When you feel that your dreams are too big to achieve, look for smaller things to accomplish in the meantime. Even big achievers started small.

*I*sn't there is a lot of excitement in the air? And not just because you feel it right now, but because it's always there.

*I*t's never too late to start something new, just as it's never too soon to finish what you've already begun.

$\mathcal{E}$njoy the new things in your life for as long as you can. That way they never become the old things.

When you feel uncertain about your future, make sure that your next step is firmly placed in the here and now. Trust will follow.

Spring isn't the time to worry about how others are growing but to be sure of your own direction and prepare for the summer that follows.

*W*hen starting a new part of your life, don't rush. There could be a long way to go and you wouldn't want to miss anything.

$\mathcal{S}$tand up and be proud of who you are and what you've done.

Then prepare for even better things in the future.

*T*omorrow is a good day to start making positive changes, but why wait? Today is even better.

$\mathcal{T}$he world is full of great books of knowledge and philosophy, but your body and mind are a library of all that you have done. So, learning about yourself might be the best thing you'll ever find out.

*T*ake your good feelings and run with them.

Opportunities

I have had many different opportunities in my life. Some I have taken, and great changes have followed. Others I have not, and regret and sometimes relief have followed. But whether I take an opportunity or not, I always thank life for giving me the right to choose.

*H*ow big is the universe? As vast as you allow it to be.

This could be the day when your destiny presents itself. Don't just stand there – get on board!

*G*ood fortune doesn't come to those who think it will, it comes to those who feel it will.

The spirit of life is in all living beings. Recognize this and you will feel limitless; ignore it and you will become small-minded and contained.

Open up to life!

*N*ow is the time to look for possibilities. That way, you give them permission to occur.

$\mathcal{T}$his life is made for you and you are certainly made for it.

*O*pportunities come for a reason. Don't waste time asking why they are there – act.

*G*ood things may come to those who wait, but they will come much more quickly to those who are motivated.

There are many things in life that can make us feel small, chiefly our own mind. And yet our mind is as limited as we make it. Expand your horizons!

*W*e all have a much more highly evolved part of us than we know. Too many of us leave it behind when we wake up in the morning.

*T*ime is only a measurement;
it's what we do with it that is
important.

If you have to tell yourself that tomorrow's another day then you really haven't finished this one.

*P*eople say that life is to be enjoyed to the full. Don't just say it – get involved!

There are many things we don't know about the universe – and even more to discover about ourselves.

*M*ake the most of life. Be all you can be and nothing you shouldn't.

*I*t's good to realize your potential every day, but don't stop there, take it to the next level.

$\mathcal{T}$he forces of nature are in the world to move and shape life; shape your own life with the force of nature that is your attitude.

The world is waking up and so must you.

$\mathcal{I}$t's understandable to shy away from danger, but unfulfilling to shy away from a challenge.

You can't command the universe to bring you things that you want, but you can ask it nicely for the things you need.

$\mathcal{D}$on't just sit and let life pass you by, follow it and see where it leads you.

*Y*ou already possess everything you need to get through this life.

If you don't know that then it's time to wake up what's inside you.

Change

I have learned that change is an everyday occurrence. Even though most days bring only the smallest of differences to my life, I am aware that there are always changes taking place. Now that I know this, the bigger changes seem less ominous!

*L*ife is changing. Don't tell me you've only just noticed!

The passing seasons are a reminder that there are always more changes to come in life. Get in line with them and with your true purpose.

*C*hange occurs every moment of every day, so it shouldn't be a hard thing to accept.

So many new things appear in the springtime, but most have been here before. What part of yourself would you like to see again?

$\mathcal{I}$f you often think that change will bring you unhappiness then the first change you need to make is how you think.

*S*pring is the right time to clear out all the stuff that has been hanging around doing nothing. That is because it reminds us that it's OK to let go.

*L*ife is always full of changes. If you strengthen your attitude, you can learn to make them work for you.

*T*omorrow hasn't arrived yet, so why waste time or thought on it?

Live every moment and reality will reveal itself.

*W*hen you start to notice wonderful changes in other people, it could just be that you're catching your own reflection. Well done!

*Y*ou have endured many changes just to stay part of this life. You are wiser just because you have come this far. Whether you know it or not, you are stronger and more beautiful too.

So, it's worth the struggle. Persevere.

*T*ake it easy – things are going just as they should. Stress is just an inner storm and like all storms it will blow over.

*D*eath can never be seen as the end of a life lived to the full.

$\mathcal{S}$pringtime shows us that everything returns to life when it is nurtured by a higher source. We are guided by that same force, so don't worry.

*D*eath only really affects the living and only the living can die. There's something bigger here that always seems to go unnoticed...

Growth

I'm not the tallest person in the world, but I've never stopped growing and learning new things, especially in areas I thought I'd already learned a lot about! Now I realize that when I think I know enough about something, I'm actually limiting my growth. If only I'd thought like this in my teens, maybe now I'd be over six feet tall!

$\mathcal{I}$t has been said that it's not where you start, but where you finish that is important. That's true, but never ignore what happens in between.

*I*f life has given you challenges, be grateful for them. Isn't that why some people grow more than others?

Wake up and smell the karma.

$\mathcal{D}$arkness is always followed by light, just as every problem has a solution.

*T*he heart that has been touched by both sadness and joy is a strong heart, made even stronger by the understanding that both were necessary for growth.

*P*ositive thinking strengthens the attitude. A strong positive attitude will help you overcome anything.

*R*ain may be discouraging, but never forget that it encourages growth and that dark clouds will eventually be followed by sunshine.

*H*eavy days and troubled nights mean we need to take charge of our mind. Then we will be in control.

$\mathscr{E}$ven when we are faced with the most difficult problems we must understand that as long as we are facing them we are alive – and where there's life, there's hope.

The best course of action is always the one we learn most from.

*H*indsight can be a wonderful teacher, but those who don't have to look back are their own masters.

$\mathcal{B}$e responsible for all you do and all you say. That means knowing what you are doing and what you are talking about.

$\mathcal{B}$elief often leaves us with many doubts.

Go beyond belief and be sure.

*I*f you still have hurdles to get over, that's good: it means that you haven't finished living.

*L*ife can be tough, but what's the alternative?

Understanding and forgiveness will lift you above the pains of the past and allow you to avoid the problems of tomorrow.

*C*an you do more to improve yourself? If you think you can, you've already started.

*I*t's much better not to have a temper than to lose it.

*T*hose who put effort into their lives always succeed, even if their goals change along the way. So, just keep trying.

*W*hen you feel that life is an uphill struggle, just wait until you see the view from the top.

*D*on't allow tiredness to become exhaustion, or irritation to become anger. It's your space, so you're responsible for what happens in it.

$\mathcal{T}$oo many people give up their dreams for fear of failure. Imagine how many people are stuck in fear! Keep moving forward regardless.

Try to give up the need to always be right; instead, just try to be.

*O*vercoming adversity is something we were all born to do. Not because we want to, but because we have to.

*B*e in control of what you put into each new day. Don't allow fear to take it from you.

*L*ife is bursting out of the earth. It does that to remind us to keep going.

$\mathcal{B}$eauty isn't necessarily in the eye of the beholder. Use all of your senses and recognize it on a much higher level.

*H*ow you think can change your mood. How you react can shape your life. Who you are can take a long time to discover.

But it's worth the effort.

*W*hat is heaven and what is hell?
Neither exists unless you create it.

It's your call.

Pause

I'm amazed when I look back at my life how much of a rush I always seemed to be in. I was terrible for trying to accomplish in a day what should have taken at least a week. I don't know what I thought I would get as a reward! But whenever I had a moment I would think of more things to do to fill the time. I moved home six times in ten years, and I don't think I can remember what one of those homes felt like. What was the point of that?!

*T*he still mind is clear and prepared.

What is it prepared for?

Absolutely anything.

The world has many beauty spots, but they are only seen by those whose eyes are truly open.

Look around you.

*T*ell yourself what you really want out of life and then stop and ask yourself what you really need.

$\mathcal{I}$f you find that life is confusing and the answers won't come to you, maybe it's time to stop and look at the questions you're asking.

$\mathcal{M}$otion and stillness are both important when used at the appropriate moment.

$\mathcal{T}$ake a minute to look back on your accomplishments and tell yourself that you're doing well. That will give you permission to accomplish more.

*M*editation and contemplation are the mind's resting place, a chance to recharge and replenish.

*W*hen things seem as though they are falling apart, be still, and in your stillness calm the motion.

*L*isten to your inner voice – the one that says, *I told you that would happen.*

Be at one with it and you'll never need to hear it again.

*G*oing slowly helps you take in all that surrounds you, through sight, taste, touch, smell, and hearing, but remember that all these wonderful senses direct their messages to your heart so that you can feel what's around you.

When things become too much and people around you have only negative, fearful views of the world, stop and clear your mind, and recognize that we all see the world through different eyes. Look for better things.

*E*veryone has an angel to guide them, so when you are feeling down, remember to look up.

If you live in the moment then reality becomes certain; if you live in your head, full of thoughts of uncertainty, then where actually are you?

$\mathcal{B}$e aware of the atmosphere that surrounds you. If you aren't, others will be.

*W*henever you feel uncertain about the future, gather yourself in the here and now. It's better to be sure of where you are than unsure of something that hasn't happened.

*N*ature's gifts are free, but don't abuse them, or, worse, ignore them.

Why not stop and look around you?

When big decisions are in front of you, take a moment and remind yourself that all this will soon be behind you. Nothing is permanent.

*D*o you feel that you are in a storm? Be still and let it rage around you. The winds are there to blow your mind free of confusion and help you to see clearly.

Clarity makes for good decisions.

*N*ow is the time to stop and do a reality check.

Take in all that is real at this moment and know that you are where you are supposed to be.

Now, what next?

*T*ake a minute to pause and appreciate all you have been through on your life's journey.

Knowing where you've been is a good indicator of where you still have to go.

*W*henever you feel lost or uncertain about your life, just know that above you there is a guiding light who wants to help. Never be afraid to ask.

*I*t is very compassionate to put others before you in life; it is foolish to do it without cause.

Love

It takes a long time for any of us to know even a little about love, even when we are in it, or feel it for others or for ourselves. The older I become, the more I realize love is like the tide coming and going through my life, and that if I stand still and stop looking, it will rush back to me at some point. When it engulfs me, I will enjoy every minute of it and I won't be sad to see it go, because I am certain it will come back.

If you're looking for love and having trouble finding it, why not look inside yourself?

*K*indness opens the heart to love. So don't wait for others to be kind – be kind to yourself.

*N*ot a day goes by when we don't think of love.

Don't let one go by without feeling it.

Why go out looking for a soul mate if you don't know what your soul actually is? Time for a bit of soul-searching maybe?

*T*he space between friends is filled with joy; the space in their hearts is filled with love.

*T*his is a day to tell people who care about you what you feel. Not what you think, but what is really happening inside.

How deep is your love for another? As deep as it is for yourself.

Making new friends and acquaintances is easy when true sharing is your intention.

*I*t has been said that it's better to give than to receive. In fact, it's good to do both – it makes us more complete.

Mother Nature presents us with an amazing array of color, beauty, and wondrous things. Now would be a good time to thank her for the gifts she has given.

*I*f all of life is interconnected, we can never be alone.

*W*alk tall with grace and dignity
in every step you take and life will
reward you with kindness, goodness,
and love.

*N*othing is worth hating for, but everything is worth loving for.

If you are as hard on yourself as you are on others, isn't it time to remember kindness?

*L*ove is always just a thought away,
so don't get down, get thinking.

*M*emories of love are treasures of the mind. Like any treasure, they shouldn't be locked away – they are yours to admire whenever you feel the need.

*L*ove is a constant like the air we breathe; without it we wouldn't exist.

*T*o share is a good thing. Be open to sharing and you will create a flow of give and take.

*I*f home is where the heart is, why not make it safe, warm, and welcoming?

When you truly have love in your heart and are sure about yourself, then when it comes to decisions, fear isn't an option.

*G*et to know yourself spiritually and then you can relax, because you will know that life goes on forever and love never really dies.

*L*ove and life are connected, they follow each other around, and without one, the other wouldn't exist.

Think how lucky you are — you have both.

$\mathcal{L}$earn to love – it's why you're here.

*I*t is difficult to watch a friend or loved one suffer; it is even more difficult when you feel their pain. But remember, if you can feel what they are feeling you are carrying some of the burden.

*T*o die is to be reborn, and to be reborn is to recognize life.

And when we recognize life, we recognize love... and know that it is eternal.

No need to rush then.

The physical heart is filled with blood that allows us to live; the spiritual heart is filled with love that allows us to live forever.

Happiness

When I was young I used to associate happiness with laughter, but now I know that it's more to do with contentment.

Now isn't that a funny thing?

$\mathcal{D}$on't allow fears of the future to hold you back – dance in the light of the here and now.

*H*ighs and lows will present themselves many times in your life. Experience both, but aim for contentment.

*I*f you want to feel good about yourself, get out into nature. It's your God-given right.

This is a good day to be ridiculously happy about your life. It doesn't matter what's going on in it, just be happy!

Happiness is all around you.
Open your heart and mind and pull
it into your life.

*W*hat makes you feel good? If you know the answer, go and get some!

This is a great day to tell yourself that life is good. No matter what obstacles are in front of you, just know that they will soon be behind you.

$\mathcal{G}$ive yourself permission to have
the greatest day of your life.

Isn't it great to be your own boss?

*L*ighten your mind and you will lighten your day and probably someone else's as well. Remember the law of cause and effect.

So many people are running in so many directions but achieving little. If you can see this then you aren't one of them, but are in the right place. Be happy.

*I*f you always make the best of yourself, speak with consideration, and mean what you say, you will always get attention for the right reasons.

Today is a great day to pat yourself on the back and feel proud. Why? Because you have already come this far.

*Y*our body works well when your heart beats steadily; your mind works well when it knows peace. Balance comes when body and mind are in harmony.

*W*ho would know if you didn't exist? Certainly not you, so go out and make a noise! Sometimes it feels good to be seen and heard.

*N*o matter what chaos is going on around you, this can still be a beautiful day if you tell yourself it is.

Telling yourself the day is beautiful gives new life to possibilities.

People spend so much money on making themselves look and feel better.

Put a smile on your face – it's free and does more good.

*C*an you truly say that you are where you should be right now? If you are, you won't have to say anything.

*A*lways remember the best part of yourself, even when you don't think that you amount to much. Reaffirming that you have done good things will attract goodness to you.

*Y*ou can never lose time if you're on the right path; being on the right path means you're contented right now.

*Y*ou don't need to look much further than yourself to find happiness – remember it's a feeling, not an object.

*C*an you achieve anything greater than peace, love, and contentment?

How about all three at once?

$\mathcal{E}$very living being has a spirit, which means that every living being has an inner light.

Imagine how bright the world would be if every living being knew that... and shone.

JOIN THE HAY HOUSE FAMILY

As the leading self-help, mind, body and spirit publisher in the UK, we'd like to welcome you to our family so that you can enjoy all the benefits our website has to offer.

 EXTRACTS from a selection of your favourite author titles

 COMPETITIONS, PRIZES & SPECIAL OFFERS Win extracts, money off, downloads and so much more

 LISTEN to a range of radio interviews and our latest audio publications

 CELEBRATE YOUR BIRTHDAY An inspiring gift will be sent your way

 LATEST NEWS Keep up with the latest news from and about our authors

 ATTEND OUR AUTHOR EVENTS Be the first to hear about our author events

 iPHONE APPS Download your favourite app for your iPhone

 HAY HOUSE INFORMATION Ask us anything, all enquiries answered

join us online at **www.hayhouse.co.uk**

  292B Kensal Road, London W10 5BE
T: 020 8962 1230 E: info@hayhouse.co.uk

ABOUT THE AUTHOR

Photographer: Angela Nott

Gordon Smith has been hailed as 'the UK's best medium', and is renowned for his astonishing ability to pinpoint exact names of people, places, and even streets relevant to a person's life.

From early childhood, Gordon had the ability to see, sense, and hear spirit people. At the age of 24, he embarked on 15 years of study and practice, going on to develop his abilities as a medium – or messenger from the spirit world – under the tutelage of some of the great legends of the spiritualist church. Gordon is now a bestselling author and one of the world's top psychic mediums and spiritual teachers, conducting mediumship workshops and events around the world. His Celtic charm and lively demonstrations – delivered in his trademark style combining humor, pure passion, and empathy toward others – provide his audiences with a rare opportunity to experience the fascinating phenomenon of mediumship.

www.gordonsmithmedium.com
www.psychicviews.co.uk